Deliverance from Negative Dreams and Nightmares by Force: Powerful Prayers for Breaking the Spell of Demonic Dreams & Stopping Nightmares and Bad Dreams

PIUS JOSEPH © 2019 All Rights Reserved

The facts herein provided are truthful in all its entirety and coherent, in that no legal responsibility, in the form of consideration or else by the use or misuse of any teaching or directions contained within shall lie against the author.

The information offered here is for the purposes of spiritual uplifting and growth only. The author is aware that the application of this book may differ from one person to another as such things as faith, trust, purity, and consistency can determine the outcomes that you receive from the application of the principles in this book.

Unless otherwise indicated, all scriptural quotations are taken from the King James Version © 1988-2007 Bible Soft Inc.

TABLE OF CONTENTS

Who Needs these Prayers? 5
    Part 1 .... *8*
Negative Dreams and Nightmares 8

CHAPTER 1 1

CHAPTER 2 4

Where Dreams & Nightmares Come from? 4
Simple Ways to Influence Your Dream/Prevent
Nightmares 7

CHAPTER 3 9

Dream Controllers/Nightmares 9
Pick of the day 9
Spiritual Study 11
The Tool of Messages 17
Satan's Doorway to Your Dreams 18
Portals 21
Sin and iniquity 23
Unforgiveness 31
What You Should Do To Your Dreams Every Day 33

CHAPTER 4 38

Defeating the Spirit of Negative Dream/Nightmares 38
Mentality 48
The word 50
Too Much Respect for Nightmares and Bad Dreams 55
    Part 2 .... *59*

Prayers 59

CHAPTER 5 60

Violent Prayers for Handling Negative Dreams and Nightmares 60
Prayer for Mercies 62
Prayer for God's Protection of Fire 72
Prayers for Deliverance by Force 74
Enforcing peaceful night Rest 78
Binding the Spirit of Fear and Disfavour 80
Prayer of appreciation 85

Who Needs these Prayers?

This book is for all those who have been experiencing either one of the following situations in their lives:

Have you been seen lions or dogs or strange animals chasing you in the dream? Do you have sex while you are sleeping? Do you eat during your dreams? Do you have sleep paralysis or see all types of satanic vision shortly before you fall asleep. Do you wake up from sleep with your heart racing? Do you talk while you are sleeping? Do you wake up with anxiety and a lot of fear? Do you have general bad dreams and Nightmares? These are all signs of demonic oppression that comes through dreams and nightmares.

If you visit your doctor and tell him some of the symptoms that you experience, he may recommend some drugs for you in order to help you out. But I can tell you that no amount of drugs can stop demonic oppression in dreams or nightmares. The greatest remedy for them is to use the word of God and prayer in order to destroy their strongholds in your life. If no step is taking in this direction, you can continue to take drugs and remain under heavy demonic oppression in your dreams or nightmares.

Thankfully, believers have the authority through the name of Jesus to cast out every demon of oppressive dreams and nightmares. Once you apply the name of Jesus are your authority in the name of Jesus and cut off the roots of the demons that sponsor those dreams and nightmares, you will notice that your dream will become very peaceful. It is this lack of understanding that has left many in bondage not knowing that they are entitled to a sound sleep every night they go to bed. The Bible says my people perish for lack of knowledge.

I present to you this Holy Ghost inspired book that will help you take authority over every spirit of nightmares and negative dreams. It is a book that will ensure your deliverance by force and by fire. Whether the devil likes it or not, his tenure in your dreams and nightmares has expired.

Be open-hearted as you read this book. Allow the spirit of God to lead you as to when to pray the prayers contained in this book. If the spirit of God is leading you to pray these prayers in the night season, please do as led. If the Holy Spirit is leading you to follow the prayer watches, do not struggle with him but pray the prayers as the Holy Spirit leads you. I am waiting for your testimonies.

Yours in Christ,

Pius Joseph

Part 1

Negative Dreams and Nightmares

Pius Joseph

CHAPTER 1

Throughout Scriptures, one of the ways which God uses to communicate to his children is dreams. As you sleep, God gives you a divine direction in your dream or even tell you what you should do in your dreams. So the devil uses contaminated dreams and nightmares to prevent the believer from receiving messages from God.

While the word of God that you study is food for your life, the devil will try to feed you with contaminated food in your dream in order to defile you.

Negative Dreams and Nightmares

Matthew 4:4

> ***But he answered and said, It is written, Man shall not live by bread alone, but by every word that proceedeth out of the mouth of God.***

The Bible makes us understand that man is not supposed to live by bread alone but by every word that proceeds out of the mouth of God. It means that either physical bread or the word that proceeds from the mouth of God can sustain a man.

This is the reason why the devil comes in the dream of many believers to feed them with negative food in their dreams. It is very obvious why the devil does that because he has an agenda to carry out in the life of that man. There are many people who ate in dreams and woke up with cancer. Some people have eaten in the dream and woke up with different kinds of sicknesses. Some ate in the dream and when they woke from sleep, their spiritual fervency died. The plan of the devil is to destroy a man through what he eats in the dream.

Am I trying to scare you? No! Just to let you know that your dreams ought to be taken very seriously. Whenever there is an attack in that area, it must be dealt with immediately through extensive prayer and the word of God.

CHAPTER 2

Where Dreams & Nightmares Come from?

It is not all dreams that come from the devil. Several factors can influence the dream of the night. Although we are not ignorant of the devices of the devil because he can also use dreams to attack a believer. But not all dreams come from the devil. From Scripture, we can see that God also uses the dream to speak to his children. It is also possible for your dreams to be a product of your physical activities during the day. If you carried out several activities in the daytime, the activities that were performed during the conscious hours can become the fulcrum of your night dreams.

Knowing this will save you from making wrong assumptions and binding the devil when there is none to bind. The activities or business that becomes the centre of your thoughts in the day, can become the central theme of your dream at night.

While eating in dream, negative dreams, and nightmares are generally bad, some dreams are offshoots of your activities in the daytime.

Ecclesiastes 5:3

> ***For a dream cometh through the multitude of business; and a fool's voice is known by multitude of words.***

Negative Dreams and Nightmares

For instance, a believer who was busy in the day barbecuing shouldn't be surprised if he finds himself dreaming about barbecuing and feasting in the dream of the night. To bind the devil in that kind of circumstance will be a waste of time. That dream may not be indicative of demonic oppression or attack. Except if the dream causes:

Sickness

Physical weakness

Depression

Disfavour and disappointment

Severe fear

Anxiety, worry, and panic

Besides that, your dreams could be the flurry of activities which you did on a particular day.

Pius Joseph

Simple Ways to Influence Your Dream/Prevent Nightmares

From the book of Ecclesiastes 5 versus three which we saw, it is actually possible to determine the kind of dream you have every night. You can overcome the spirit of bad dreams and nightmares by following a pattern of activity in the day. It is unreasonable for a person who says that he is a child of God to go through the entire day without storing anything in his spiritual bank account. The more stock your daily activities with God, the better you are able to take control of your night dreams.

Dreams come through multitudes of activities in the day. Everything that you do in a day can become the source of your dream in the night. By taking charge of your day with spiritually enhancing activities, you can actually determine what kind of dream you have in the night when you sleep. Never

Negative Dreams and Nightmares

allow a day to pass by without actually carrying out some spiritual task. A spiritually rich day is essential to a spiritually rich dream.

CHAPTER 3

Dream Controllers/Nightmares

We will examine some things that you can do in the day that will affect your dream. Since what you do can be a window to your night dreams.

Pick of the day

I recommend you get a Journal. Every day, pick a particular spiritual activity that you know is necessary for you to do. Your dream is influenced by the kind of activities you do

Negative Dreams and Nightmares

during the day. The more spiritualise your day, the better your dreams will be. For instance, if you decide that you want to meditate on the word of God, meditate until your mind is saturated with God's word.

Joshua 1:8

> *This book of the law shall not depart out of thy mouth; but thou shalt meditate therein day and night, that thou mayest observe to do according to all that is written therein: for then thou shalt make thy way prosperous, and then thou shalt have good success.*

Meditation can influence the type of dreams that you have. Meditating on the word of

God has many benefits such as light, the enlightenment of the heart, good success, et cetera. There is a difference between success and good success. A person might be successful yet lack peace. That isn't the kind of success that the Bible is talking about. Good success is like God blessing you and the blessings that he has given you will add you no sorrow.

Spiritual Study

A diligent and engaging study of the word of God does not only influence your dream, but it also controls your dreams. Sometimes our dreams are a reflection of the dominant things that occupy our minds and even the things that we do. If the spiritual becomes the pursuit of your day, it will become the platform for your dreams. One day I read about eighty chapters of the Bible. I read the chapters of the Bible until my spirit man became saturated in the word of God. In the

Negative Dreams and Nightmares

night, I found myself dreaming about the chapters of the Bible I had read during the day. Even if you don't have to read your hardcopy Bible, there are Bibles in different platforms that are available for you. You can have the Bible playing on your phone so that it can get into your spirit man. When you do that the word of God in your spirit man will give no room to the devil to come and attack your dreams or give you nightmares. If a dream can take the dimension of your physical activity. You should, therefore, consider filling your daily activities with one form of spiritual exercise or the other.

And the devil is never tired of attacking believers in the dream of the night. The main focus of the enemy's attack in dreams or nightmares is to cause fear, rejection, affliction or illnesses, spiritual bondage, spiritual lethargy, spiritual defeat, et cetera.

Pius Joseph

There are some believers whose primary way of communicating with God is through dreams. They may not be hearing the voice of God in their ear or in their spirit man, but they are no stranger to the voice of God in their dreams. Such people can sleep and have several dreams where God gives them divine direction. Every time their head touches the bed or the pillow in the night, a deluge of dreams will be raining on them. That is their own way of interacting with God. When Satan decides to fill their night with terrible dreams and nightmares, he may block that way of divine direction which they have in their sleep.

Joseph, the husband of Mary, received all his divine direction through dreams.

Matthew 2:13

> ***And when they were departed, behold, the angel of the Lord***

Negative Dreams and Nightmares

> ***appeareth to Joseph in a dream, saying, Arise, and take the young child and his mother, and flee into Egypt, and be thou there until I bring thee word: for Herod will seek the young child to destroy him.***

It is when he is sleeping that God will appear to him in the dream of the night and tell him this is what you should do and this is what you shouldn't do. Even though the life of Jesus was at stake, God was in no hurry to talk to Joseph through other means of direction. He would allow Joseph to go to bed and by night appear to him either by an angel or some other means. Even when Pharaoh wanted to have the baby Jesus slain, it was an angel that appeared to Joseph in the dream and told him to flee into Egypt because

Pius Joseph

Pharaoh will make a determined effort in order to destroy the life of the baby.

Matthew 2:19-21

> *But when Herod was dead, behold, an angel of the Lord appeareth in a dream to Joseph in Egypt,*
>
> *20 Saying, Arise, and take the young child and his mother, and go into the land of Israel: for they are dead which sought the young child's life.*
>
> *21 And he arose, and took the young child and his mother, and came into the land of Israel.*

Negative Dreams and Nightmares

Throughout Scriptures, dreams remain one of the ways that God uses to talk to his people. But the enemy uses dreams and nightmares to attack believers so that instead of the believer hearing God when he sleeps, he is busy eating in the dream, having sex in the dream, having different kinds of animals or strange beasts pursuing him, and all manner of negative things that happen in the night. As a result, the believer may miss the voice of God or the divine direction that God has for him. Any attack upon your dream life is something that should not be treated with levity it must be violently rejected because the devil has no right to trespass upon your dream. Just as the Bible says, this is the day that the Lord has made. That is the same thing that you should say to your night, this is the night that the Lord has made. And if the Lord has made the night, then the devil has no right whatsoever to trespass upon your sleep.

Pius Joseph

The Tool of Messages

Messages and other tools are things you can use to control your dreams. The spirit of man does not sleep even though your flesh may be sleeping. Your spirit is active. That is why it is possible to have dreams because if your spirit man was asleep, it would have been impossible for you to have dreams and nightmares. By playing something very lightly in the background, you are able to tell your spirit man what it should listen to. However, there are some people who do not want any iota of noise when they are sleeping. For such people, you can use other means of dream controllers to influence the type of dreams you have in the night. But if you can accommodate an audio Bible or messages playing while you are sleeping, it is a very good tool for controlling the type of dreams you have in the night.

Negative Dreams and Nightmares

Satan's Doorway to Your Dreams

Before Satan can do anything contrary to the child of God, he needs the permission of God or the permission of the child of God. We saw this played out in the life of Job when Satan had to approach God and sought for consent before he attacked this man of God.

Job 1:7-12

> *7 And the Lord said unto Satan, Whence comest thou? Then Satan answered the Lord, and said, From going to and fro in the earth, and from walking up and down in it.*
>
> *8 And the Lord said unto Satan, Hast thou considered my servant*

Job, that there is none like him in the earth, a perfect and an upright man, one that feareth God, and escheweth evil?

9 Then Satan answered the Lord, and said, Doth Job fear God for nought?

10 Hast not thou made an hedge about him, and about his house, and about all that he hath on every side? thou hast blessed the work of his hands, and his substance is increased in the land.

11 But put forth thine hand now, and touch

Negative Dreams and Nightmares

> *all that he hath, and he will curse thee to thy face.*
>
> *12 And the Lord said unto Satan, Behold, all that he hath is in thy power; only upon himself put not forth thine hand. So Satan went forth from the presence of the Lord.*

And God wouldn't give the devil any permission to attack you in your dreams or give you nightmares because it would be contrary to the word of God in the book of Psalms 127:2

> *It is vain for you to rise up early, to sit up late, to eat the bread of sorrows: for so he*

Pius Joseph

giveth his beloved sleep.

If the Lord will give you a peaceful sleep, why then will he give permission to the enemy to attack you by terrible dreams and nightmares? That will be diametrically opposed to the nature and the character of God.

However, most of the encounters of dreams and nightmares could be either as a result of demonic oppression or the believer might have open the door for the enemy to come in. We will discuss some of those common doors that a believer may mistakenly or otherwise open to the enemy in order for negative dreams or nightmares to gain expression in the sleep of the believer.

Portals

A demonic portal is an opening that the devil uses to cause destruction in the life of a

Negative Dreams and Nightmares

believer. Once the devil finds such a portal, he will continue to make use of that portal to afflict the believer and oppress him. Several reasons can be adduced for the opening of satanic portals in the life of a believer. I know this is a prayer book, but at least, I should take some time to explain certain things to you in order to ensure that before you pray the root causes of your negative dreams and nightmares are dealt with. Of what use is your prayer to cast out the demon of negative dreams and nightmares when the root cause of that dream has not been dealt with. It is like a man who has an internal injury but decided to treat it superficially. As long as that internal injury has not been healed, he will continue to suffer pains. So we need to deal with the root causes of demonic portals so that our prayers will be effective.

An individual can be suffering from severe demonic attack without actually knowing where the source of the opening is coming from. It is not every time that you experience an attack in your dream, oppression, or nightmares that you just go straight and begin to bind the devil. Sometimes, it may not be the devil but a door that you might have mistakenly or unconsciously open to the devil. If you have been careless with what you feed your eyes or even the things you hear, it is possible that it can become the source of the demonic nightmares or bad dreams. A believer who is used to watching violent films or horror movies shouldn't be surprised if he sees a big cat without a head pursuing him in the dream. By watching these kinds of movies, the believer has given the devil permission to make his sleep the devil's playing ground.

Sin and iniquity

Psalms 119:67

Negative Dreams and Nightmares

Before I was afflicted I went astray: but now have I kept thy word.

There is nothing that attracts affliction and attacks in the form of negative dreams and nightmares like sin and iniquity. From the Scripture under reference, we can see that the psalmist was saying before he was afflicted, he went astray. So the affliction came because he strayed away. In the absence of straying away, there can be no affliction. One day, God gave me an instruction not to sleep at that time. I heard that instruction clearly, but in disobedience, I turned in and slept. I was terribly afflicted in the dream and oppressed that I woke up very angry with the Lord why he didn't protect me. You know that time, I was still a baby Christian and didn't know the spiritual implication of getting angry with the Lord.

Pius Joseph

As my face was contorted by anger, I heard the Lord said to me, "every time you disobey me, Satan has the right to attack you."

What an important lesson this communicated to my spirit. Sin and iniquity open a gate to the enemy to oppress the believer with bad dreams or nightmares. You see, it was because of the sin of disobedience that the enemy was able to oppress me in my dream. If I hadn't sinned, he wouldn't have had the inroad to come against me in my dream. A transient measure won't be enough to deal with any sin and iniquity. You may need to take steps to deal with the sin from its roots.

Matthew 15:13

> ***But he answered and said, Every plant, which my heavenly Father hath not***

Negative Dreams and Nightmares

planted, shall be rooted up.

The Scripture says every tree that my father has not planted shall be removed from its roots. Even God knows that issues are properly dealt with when their source is destroyed. If you decide to adopt a temporary measure, it will only halt the activities of the enemy for that period. If you want to permanently lay to rest the attacks of the enemy in that direction, you must deal with it from the roots by removing any source of sin.

Friends, a lot of folks have been praying against the attacks of the enemy in bad dreams or nightmares, but they don't want to handle the main cause of the problem. When the children of Israelites opened their lives to sin, the enemies usually have a free day of operation – destroying both them and their crops. As they dwelt in this life of iniquity and sin, they were exposed to severe enemy hostility. But once they repent from their sins, the Lord defends them. He protects them from the enemy's onslaughts.

No matter how God loves you, he can't defend you if you live in sin.

Ecclesiastes 10:8

> ***He that diggeth a pit shall fall into it; <u>and whoso breaketh an hedge, a serpent shall bite him</u>.***

Iniquity and sin weaken your spiritual shield and defence. The more you live in sin, the lesser your defence against the enemy will be. The sin and iniquity you allow may not be unrelated to what you are currently experiencing in your dreams and nightmares. Beloved, don't just bind the

Negative Dreams and Nightmares

devil, examine your life carefully to see if you have opened the door to the devil.

Gladly, you don't have to continue to remain in your sin any longer. The Bible says God's desire for every child of God is to live above sin. Yet if any man sins, we have an advocate with the Father Jesus Christ the righteous who have been offered as a sacrifice for our sins and also for the sin of the whole world (1 John 2:1-2). All you need to do is to go before the Lord and ask for mercy and he will forgive you. And trust Him for the grace not to return back to the same sin again. When David sinned by committing murder and fornication, he repented and God forgave him. And David's repentance was genuine because he never went back to the same sin again. You can check through the entire Bible to see whether David committed that type of sin. At the final phase of David's life, the devil was still struggling to make a statement that David's repentance was not genuine.

The men that were with David brought a fair damsel, Abishag the Shunamite, yet David the King declined to touch her. It shows that his repentance was genuine.

1 Kings 1:1-4

> *Now king David was old and stricken in years; and they covered him with clothes, but he gat no heat.*
>
> *2 Wherefore his servants said unto him, Let there be sought for my lord the king a young virgin: and let her stand before the king, and*

Negative Dreams and Nightmares

let her cherish him, and let her lie in thy bosom, that my lord the king may get heat.

3 So they sought for a fair damsel throughout all the coasts of Israel, and found Abishag a Shunammite, and brought her to the king.

4 And the damsel was very fair, and cherished the king, and ministered to him: but the king knew her not.

All the devil requires in order to terrify you by negative dreams and nightmares is just a small opening or a door. However small the door might be, when he gains entrance into your life, he can wreck a lot of havoc.

Unforgiveness

I want to resist the temptation of giving you only the prayers you need to pray in order to get free from bad dreams and nightmares. But the reason why we need to talk about some of these issues is simple. If they are left unresolved, Satan can still gain access into your dreams and terrify you by nightmares. A lot of people have temporary deliverance from satanic oppression. One day or two months they are free from demonic attacks and oppression in their lives. And the next moment, they are under heavy demonic oppressions again. Whenever the devil has been cast out and he returns back again, he comes with a lot of demons in order to ensure that the believer doesn't gain freedom anymore.

Luke 11:26

Negative Dreams and Nightmares

> ***Then goeth he, and taketh to him seven other spirits more wicked than himself; and they enter in, and dwell there: and the last state of that man is worse than the first.***

This matter of unforgiveness is serious to the extent that the Bible says even if you have a gift to offer to the Lord and you remember that there is someone you need to reconcile and forgive, leave your gift on the altar go back and reconcile then come back and offer your gift to the Lord.

Matthew 5:23

> ***Therefore if thou bring thy gift to the altar, and there rememberest that thy***

brother hath ought against thee;

24 Leave there thy gift before the altar, and go thy way; first be reconciled to thy brother, and then come and offer thy gift.

The sin of unforgiveness will not only hinder you from having access to God, but it will also make all the prayers in this book useless and ineffective.

What You Should Do to Your Dreams Every Day

Every time you wake up from a negative dream, the first thing to do before you begin the activities of your day is to cancel that dream immediately in the name of Jesus. There is power in the name of Jesus, so you

Negative Dreams and Nightmares

may need to rebuke that devil that came in your dream. You have the authority to decree things and they will come to pass. Handle those dreams by stopping them from coming to pass immediately.

It the dream that you had in the night is about a particular food that you ate, the moment you wake up, neutralise the effect of that dream in the name of Jesus. Learn to use your authority concerning your dreams.

If the attacks become too frequent, you may need to cover your dreams with the blood of Jesus before you go to bed.

Revelation 11:12

> *11 And they overcame him by the blood of the Lamb, and by the word of their testimony; and they loved not*

their lives unto the death.

This will restrain every satanic invasion of your dreams.

The Bible says to stand still and know that he is God. The plan of the devil is to terrify you by dreams. So that each time you go to bed, you are so afraid that the enemy would attack you by feeding you with his own food through your dreams or give you a bad dream or nightmare

For all intents and purposes, the devil wants to ensure that you remain a victim of his dirty dreams. He desires to see you depressed when you wake up and frustrated by the dreams you have. He wants to test the faithfulness of God in your life and make you feel that God has not been answering all of your prayers. But the devil is a liar.

Negative Dreams and Nightmares

When the children of God were standing before the Red Sea, Moses told them to stand still and see the salvation of the Lord. Worrying and fretfulness are not of God. In fact, it is one of the greatest strategies of the enemy to leave you constantly under his subjection. He knows that as you continue to worry, it will be difficult for God to help you. The children of Israel had to learn this fact very early enough as they journeyed through the desert. Many believers are not utilising this weapon of battle called stillness.

Isaiah 30:15

KJV

Isa 30:15

> ***For thus saith the Lord God, the Holy One of Israel; In returning and rest shall ye be saved; in quietness***

Pius Joseph

and in confidence shall be your strength: and ye would not.

CHAPTER 4

Defeating the Spirit of Negative Dream/Nightmares

Calmness is a very potent tool for defeating the enemy in every area of your life. The devil has been and will continue to remain a disparate attention seeker. Some of the attacks of the devil are meant to get your attention and nothing more. The more he gets your attention, the more he continues to attack you by negative dreams and Nightmares. The goal of Satan here is to make sure that when the attacks of bad dreams and nightmares continue to rain on you, your attention is centred on his attacks and not on God. But calmness will always defeat him (Isaiah 30:15).

The aim of Satan is to get your attention off God and centred on himself. He does this through negative dreams and nightmares. He raises a lot of dust concerning his attacks on your life. And when he notices that he is no longer celebrated in your life, he will simply pack his bags and leave you alone.

Have you ever seen when someone is making trouble around you, and you paid no single attention to the person. The troublemaker will become so frustrated and angry that he may leave you alone. This is an aspect of a spiritual battle for defeating the enemy who is attacking you with bad dreams and nightmares. Even the Bible endorses this type of battle through calmness.

Exodus 14:13

Negative Dreams and Nightmares

And Moses said unto the people, Fear ye not, stand still, and see the salvation of the Lord, which he will shew to you to day: for the Egyptians whom ye have seen to day, ye shall see them again no more for ever.

Your calmness and your stillness is a confirmation of your trust in God. When the children of Israelites were jilted by the approaching Egyptians, and Moses himself was confused about what to do, God reminded his servant to be calm and peaceful. When you are going through difficult moments in your life and you decide to become peaceful, you are turning over the battle to the Lord. I was watching a documentary one day when I discovered that even the lions before they attacked the preys, they have a way of detecting the weakest in the animals they want to attack. It is the same technique that the devil uses. If he notices that his attacks on your life through nightmares and dreams are taking your attention or maybe making you to worry or to become depressed, he will continue to attack you in that area. Don't wake up in full panic mode because you had a bad dream or you had a nightmare. Be calm. While taking your authority over that spirit in the place of prayer, maintain a calm disposition and give no attention to the devil. I make it a habit of not even giving attention to the dream at all or even sharing it with another person.

Worry and anxiety only make the devil aware that his attacks are working. When he notices that each time you wake up from a bad dream or nightmare, and you become worried and anxious, he knows that his battle plans are yielding great results. The devil will magnify his attacks.

Negative Dreams and Nightmares

However, if you wake up from a negative dream or nightmare, and immediately you tell the devil, "you have completely wasted your time by showing yourself that dream. What you have shown yourself will come to pass against you and not me."

You can even take it to another level by refusing to pray after saying these things. You just went off and continued with the activities of your day. The devil will be wondering, is this attack working any longer? Isn't he concerned that I just attacked him?

If the devil had the power to kill you by negative dreams and nightmares, he would have done that a long time ago. I don't want this teaching to be misunderstood. The devil has no power over your life except you want to create that kind of impression. Some of the attacks the devil brings into your life are merely to get your attention and make you a captive to his attacks.

I once struggled with a negative dream. When I was suffering from that attack several years ago, I would wake up sad, angry, and depressed. I was constantly eating in my dreams and I didn't want it to proceed any further. I hated the food I ate in my dreams. When I was going through that moment of attack, it was not easy. But as I share this testimony with you, I am full of smile. If I had known what I know now, the devil wouldn't have gained a little foothold in my life. I ate all things in my dreams. I ate rice, I ate beans, fresh meat, cooked meat, all sort of meats. I ate fufu (a local Nigerian delicacy), I drank soup, I drank pap and even water. All these in my dream.

I prayed and fasted. The more I prayed, the more I ate in my dreams. And whenever I

Negative Dreams and Nightmares

woke up from my dreams, my day became miserable.

Sadness and depression would gather a formidable presence in my life, and my sadness was further compounded by the kind of things I was hearing from people. The more I hear, the angrier I became. Some of the things I was hearing engraved the spirit of fear into my life. I may need to balance this testimony at this point. Some people have eaten in their dreams and woke up with severe and terrible illnesses. So the devil can use that point to feed people with diseases. But I want you to hold onto the word of God more than the attacks of the enemy. It is the word of God that makes free and not the attacks of the enemy.

As I struggled, God was busy renovating my mentality with his word. One day, as I pondered upon all the attacks of bad dreams, a thought sailed through my mind, "if actually, the devil could kill you in the dream, he would have done that a long time ago." As these thoughts pounce on my heart, I would say that the Lord had begun the first process of my deliverance.

I thought on, "what did the Bible say about this?" Then I stumbled upon the scripture in the book of Mark 16:17 which says, "even when they drink deadly poison, it will not harm them. " That Scripture became my bosom friend. I planted myself deep in that verse even though the enemy fought very hard to throw me off that Scriptural stand. The attacks continued, but I stood on the word of God.

My deliverance was gradual. As my mentality got changed so does my attitude towards these persistent satanic attacks of bad dreams. I stopped worrying because if the devil could kill me by feeding me in the dream, I would have long been dead.

Negative Dreams and Nightmares

Depression and anxiety gone! As I no longer give attention to what the enemy was doing, he too, felt tired to continue his attacks.

The portal of my attacks had been ruined. During the process of my deliverance, I would sometimes eat in the dream but when I awoke, I simply delivered low blows to the devil, "you are wasting your time. This food you have given me is nutrition."

I was calm as ever. No worrying, no depression, and no anxiety. Before I knew it, Satan got tired of serving me his table. He was wasting it. Nothing he could do with my dreams that could fetch my attention. I was eating his food instead of being sad and depressed like I used to, I was rejoicing this time.

When I shared this testimony with a brother in Christ who also had a similar problem of eating in the dream of the night, he said each time he wakes up from bad dreams, he prayed to the Lord and convert the food to any vitamin of his choice. In his words, "I convert it to vitamin E." As the last line of his word hit my eardrum, I busted out in laughter.

I spent time changing my mindset on the word of God and it delivered me. The moment my mindset changed, my deliverance took place.

I had this testimony from God's servant Dr. Pastor Paul Enenche, the senior pastor of the Dunamis International Gospel Centre world wide. There was a pastor who was having severe and terrifying nightmares. Each time the pastor closes his eyes, he sees all kinds of animals in his dreams. Lions without head. Different types of animals chasing him in the dream of the night. One day, the pastor stumbled across a major light from Scripture. He saw in the book of Psalms 127:2, that God gives unto his children peaceful sleep. That

Negative Dreams and Nightmares

was the day the pastor received his deliverance. He said if God can give unto his children peaceful sleep, what am I doing when asleep.

Friends, some of the attacks of the enemy are meant to distract you from what you are doing. Others are meant to oppress you. No matter the intent of the devil in attacking you, calmness and peacefulness is a very potent tool in winning the battle against negative dreams and nightmares.

Mentality

The trouble with many saints of the living God is that they don't want to spend time feeding their minds with the right materials that will transform their mindset. Nobody will be able to do that for you. The obligation of consistently feeding your mind with the word that will change your story is entirely your duty. It is possible for the problem or nightmares or even the dream to still be there, but your mentality will swallow it. You will no longer see the mountain as a mighty rock, but the molehill that you can crush with a step of your feet.

What you experience was not that the devil stopped his attacks on your dreams or nightmares the devil may not have stopped, you now have an understanding that you can't be harmed by the devil's dreams or nightmares so when you wake up from a bad dream or nightmare, it doesn't bother you. The transformation has happened in your mind.

I heard the testimony of a sister who had struggled with bad dreams. Each time something good is coming her way, she would eat in the dream and that would be the end of it. That favour would never come any longer, and people who are supposed to favour her will begin to give excuses.

Negative Dreams and Nightmares

The word

There is nothing that delivers completely from the oppression of bad dreams and nightmares like the word of God. If you are too busy to open the word of God, you are too busy to be delivered. It is through the word that you can become baptised with calmness and stillness, a necessary mentality for winning the battle against bad dreams and nightmares.

It is through the word of God that you will learn that no matter what kind of dream or nightmares the devil bring your way, it can't harm you.

Isaiah 42:1-5

> *But now thus saith the Lord that created thee, O Jacob, and he that formed thee, O Israel, Fear not: for I*

have redeemed thee, I have called thee by thy name; thou art mine.

2 When thou passest through the waters, I will be with thee; and through the rivers, they shall not overflow thee: when thou walkest through the fire, thou shalt not be burned; neither shall the flame kindle upon thee.

3 For I am the Lord thy God, the Holy One of Israel, thy Saviour: I gave Egypt for thy ransom, Ethiopia and Seba for thee.

Negative Dreams and Nightmares

4 Since thou wast precious in my sight, thou hast been honourable, and I have loved thee: therefore will I give men for thee, and people for thy life.

5 Fear not: for I am with thee: I will bring thy seed from the east, and gather thee from the west;

You can't know these assurances if you are not a person of the word. How I wished I had known these things right from the beginning of the attacks of eating in the dream that I suffered, I had knocked the devil back to hell and tell him how a mighty Joker he was. But I didn't know all these things until Mark 16:17 came in handy and illuminated my life.

Pius Joseph

Many a believer don't have time for the word of God and they missed out on the opportunity to renew their mind and acquire all the tools they need to defeat the devil in battle. Some believers don't know how to fortify themselves with the word of God, and every passing attack of the enemy scares them.

I have believed and will continue to believe that the word of God is the solution to every problem of man. If you want to help anyone who is going through any situation in life don't tell them how you feel about what they are going through. Just expose them to the word of God and they will be delivered completely.

Acts 20:32

> ***And now, brethren, I commend you to God, and to the word of his grace, which is able to***

Negative Dreams and Nightmares

> ***build you up, and to give you an inheritance among all them which are sanctified.***

The word can build you up, strengthen your calmness and give you your inheritance. There are certain inalienable inheritance that are attached to your salvation in Christ Jesus. The inheritance is your possession as an heir to the kingdom of God, and it is your inheritance to sleep peacefully without any demon trying to give you a negative dream or nightmare. Yes, you have heard me right. It is your absolute inheritance. Friends, you can't know your inheritance until you have open the word of God, the Holy Bible.

Your mind must be serviced by the word of God in order to stay fit. Courage and strength are derived from the word of God as you study it and apply it to your life. The presence of fear, depression, sadness, worry, anxiety et cetera indicates that the word of God has not yet developed in our hearts.

Too Much Respect for Nightmares and Bad Dreams

Before we go into the prayer session of this book, I want to take the time to address an important issue. I am doing this without prejudice to people who have different names and interpretations of the dreams that they have. Am only trying to place the word of God above every other dream or nightmare. After all the Bible says let every man be a liar and only God be proved true. Another passage of the Bible reads as I live says the Lord every knee must bow to me and every tongue must confess that I am God. One of the main reasons why a lot of believers suffer from negative dreams and bad nightmares is because of the kind of respect that so many people have attached to

Negative Dreams and Nightmares

this kind of dreams. They tell you if you have this kind of dream, or you have this kind of nightmare, then you might have been suffering from a marine spirit. Others will tell you that if you ever it in the dream, you will have the so-so type of sickness. For some, they will tell you if you ever have this kind of nightmares, this is what you are suffering from. This has left many believers in the cage of fear when they have dreams or nightmares. I like what my spiritual father, Dr. Pastor Paul Enenche always says, that the Bible did not say that the just shall live by their dreams or nightmares, the Bible says the just shall live by faith. Let's stop the name-calling or even the so-called interpretations, some of which are way off Scriptures and keep our minds on what the word of God says. Let every man be a liar and only God be proved true.

I am not condemning interpretation of dreams or trying to make the believer understand the implication of nightmares he might have had. What I am strongly against is the exaltation of some of these bad dreams or nightmares above the word of God. As a believer in Christ Jesus, a new constitution was promulgated over your life the first day you surrendered yourself to the Lordship of Jesus Christ. This is eminently captured in the book of 2 Corinthians 5:17:

> ***Therefore if any man be in Christ, he is a new creature: old things are passed away; behold, all things are become new.***

I have suffered from this and that is why I seek to reject every form of attention that people pay to their bad dreams or nightmares that want to make it look as if the word of God is below the dreams of the devil.

Negative Dreams and Nightmares

I believe God that as your mentality and mindset change, you will receive deliverance in the mighty name of Jesus. Amen.

Part 2

Prayers

CHAPTER 5

Violent Prayers for Handling Negative Dreams and Nightmares

We have now come to an important aspect of this book. And I will encourage you not to handle this section of this book with levity. It is not for you to read through the prayers and nod your head in agreement. The prayers contained here are meant to be prayed and not read through. After the information that you have learned concerning your dreams and nightmares, it is time to pray the prayers and take that peaceful night rest that God has given to you as promised in his word by force. There are some deliverances that have to be by force. No enemy will give you his territory willingly unless you decide to use force. No wonder the Bible says you cannot go into a strong man's house and spoil his goods unless you, first of all, bind the strong man.

Matthew 12:29

> *Or else how can one enter into a strong man's house, and spoil his goods, except he first bind the strong man? and then he will spoil his house.*

Before you can safeguard your dreams, you need to bind the strong man that is making inroads and preventing you from having a peaceful sleep. For all intent and purposes, this is an active part of this book that

Negative Dreams and Nightmares

requires your prayers. As you read through the prayers contained in the pages of this book, take your time and pray them one after the other.

Prayer for Mercies

In order for you not to pray and receive no answer, we need to ask God for mercy. Without forgiveness of sins, there can be no answers to prayers that can deliver from nightmares and bad dreams.

1 John 1:9

> ***If we confess our sins, he is faithful and just to forgive us our sins, and to cleanse us from all unrighteousness.***

Psalms 66:18

Pius Joseph

If I regard iniquity in my heart, the Lord will not hear me:

Hebrews 4:15-16

For we have not an high priest which cannot be touched with the feeling of our infirmities; but was in all points tempted like as we are, yet without sin.

16 Let us therefore come boldly unto the throne of grace, that we may obtain mercy, and find grace to help in time of need.

Thank you, father, for the privilege to come before you today. I appreciate you because it

Negative Dreams and Nightmares

is only by your mercy I am able to have this privilege to talk to you. I want to confess my sins and iniquity before your throne this day and ask that the blood of your precious son will wipe them away in the name of Jesus, amen. I know that without the forgiveness of sins, there can be no answers to prayers. Your word says if I regard iniquity in my heart, you will never answer me. Therefore, I asked that you forgive me of all sins, the ones I know and the ones I don't know. Thank you mighty father because I know you have heard me, in the name of Jesus. Amen.

Dear Holy Father, your word says I should come before the throne of grace boldly in order to find mercy at this time of need. I, therefore, make demands for your mercies to cleanse me from every sin that can serve as a hindrance for my prayers right now in the name of Jesus. Cleanse and purify me wholly, body, spirit, and my soul. Thank you father, in Jesus name. Amen.

Pius Joseph

Ecclesiastes 10:8

> ***He that diggeth a pit shall fall into it; and whoso breaketh an hedge, a serpent shall bite him.***

Father in the name of Jesus, I come before you today to shut down every door that I have open to the enemy and which the devil is using to torment me in my dreams and give me terrible nightmares. Every door that the enemy has been using to afflict me in my dreams I close those doors today in the name of Jesus. Every portal that the devil has been using to attack me in my dreams I decree and declare that those portals are closed in the name of Jesus.

God Almighty, I come before you today to ask for the restoration of my hedge. Lord, I know that since the enemy has been attacking me in this manner with terrifying

Negative Dreams and Nightmares

dreams and nightmares, I must have broken the hedge in one way or the other. Your word is the truth and it cannot be compromised for anyone. You have said in your word that he that breaks the hedge, the serpent will have the authority to bite that person. Today Lord I ask that you restore my hedge that will ensure my complete defence and protection while I sleep in the night in the name of Jesus. From today, I pray that the enemy will no longer have access to me because of the restoration of the hedge which you have just done, thank you Mighty Father because this is the confidence I have in you when I ask you for anything, you do it for me.

Matthew 18:18

> ***Verily I say unto you, Whatsoever ye shall bind on earth shall be bound in heaven: and whatsoever ye shall***

Pius Joseph

loose on earth shall be loosed in heaven.

Dear Father, I want to stand today upon your word to counsel every form of satanic attacks an invasion of my dreams. You have given me the authority that whatsoever I permit here on earth, it will stand permitted. Whatsoever I forbid here on earth, it will stand forbidden even in heaven. I am standing on your own unfailing word which is settled even in the heavens. I forbid every form of attack on my dreams in the name of Jesus. I stand upon the authority of the above Scripture and I say unto the devil, from today henceforth and for the entirety of the time that I will be living on the face of the earth, you are no longer permitted to come against me in my dreams in the name of Jesus I forbid you and all your minions, in the mighty name of Jesus, amen.

Luke 10:19

Negative Dreams and Nightmares

> *Behold, I give unto you power to tread on serpents and scorpions, and over all the power of the enemy: and nothing shall by any means hurt you.*

Mark 16:17

> *They shall take up serpents; and if they drink any deadly thing, it shall not hurt them; they shall lay hands on the sick, and they shall recover.*

Father in the mighty name of Jesus, today I want to address all the spirits that have been tormenting me in my dreams and giving me nightmares. Lord, I know that behind every negative dream or nightmare, there is a spirit sponsoring it. Today, I bind every satanic or demonic spirit that is responsible for attacking me in my dreams in the mighty name of Jesus. I command you by the fire of the Holy Spirit, desist now from coming against me in my dreams in the name of Jesus. From today henceforth, I bind every form of demonic power that has been attacking my dreams by the power and the authority in the name of Jesus. Amen.

Lord, today I cast every form of demonic symbols represented by serpents, scorpions, and every form of weird animals that I see in my dreams chasing after me. From today Lord I nullify all of their activities in the mighty name of Jesus. They will no longer operate in my dreams in the name of Jesus. Amen

Exodus 12:13

> ***And the blood shall be to you for a token***

Negative Dreams and Nightmares

> *upon the houses where ye are: and when I see the blood, I will pass over you, and the plague shall not be upon you to destroy you, when I smite the land of Egypt.*

Hebrews 12:24

> *And to Jesus the mediator of the new covenant, and to the blood of sprinkling, that speaketh better things than that of Abel.*

Thank you, Lord, for the privilege to pray this prayer point. Thank you, Lord, for the sacrifice of the blood of your son that has been made available for me this day in the name of Jesus. Lord, I make demands for the

Pius Joseph

application of the blood of Jesus in my dreams today. Your word has said whenever the blood of Jesus is applied, there must be a pass over. Just as you asked the children of Israelites to apply the blood of slain animals on the doorpost of their lintels, I apply the same blood today in my dream and in my sleep in the name of Jesus. After today Lord, the enemy will no longer come near me because of the blood of Jesus in my dream and in my sleep in the mighty name of Jesus. By the power of the blood of Jesus, today marks the end of negative dreams and nightmares in the mighty name of Jesus. It ends from today in Jesus name, Amen.

Thank you, father, for the blood of your son Jesus Christ that has been made abundantly free for my deliverance. I know that by your word that the blood of your son Jesus Christ speaks better things than the blood of Abel. I make demands for the blood of Jesus to speak in my dreams while I sleep in the name of Jesus. I asked that your blood will continue to speak divine protection and a wall of fire in my dreams in the name of Jesus. Thank you, Lord, for the blood of Jesus, Amen.

Prayer for God's Protection of Fire

Hebrews 12:29

> ***For our God is a consuming fire.***

Zachariah 2:5

> ***For I, saith the Lord, will be unto her a wall of fire round about, and will be the glory in the midst of her.***

Dear Lord, I want to make demands for the application of your fire in my dreams in the name of Jesus. Your word says in the above Scriptures, that you will surround me with your ring of fire. I asked that you surround me with that same ring that will guarantee my protection against negative dreams and nightmares, in the name of Jesus. And as these things surround me today, it will mark an end to all terrifying dreams, nightmares, and everything that is contrary to your word in my dreams in the night in the name of Jesus. Thank you, father, for the ring of your fire.

Father in the name of Jesus, today I make demands for the application of the fire of the Holy Ghost upon all demonic entities and powers that oppress my dreams in the name of Jesus. I pray that the fire of the Holy Ghost consumes them today in the name of Jesus. All the works of attacks in my dreams are consumed by the fire of the Holy Spirit in the name of Jesus. Amen.

Dear Father, I make demands for the application of your fire in my dreams. The Bible says that you are a consuming fire. I ask you, father, that you consume all demonic personalities, witchcraft powers, cult powers, marine spirit, that the devil uses to attack me in my dreams in the name of Jesus. I ask that they should be consumed by fire right now in the name of Jesus.

Prayers for Deliverance by Force

Isaiah 52:2

Matthew 11:12

> ***And from the days of John the Baptist until now the kingdom of heaven suffereth violence, and the violent take it by force.***

Isaiah 10:27

> ***And it shall come to pass in that day, that***

Pius Joseph

his burden shall be taken away from off thy shoulder, and his yoke from off thy neck, and the yoke shall be destroyed because of the anointing.

Father in the name of Jesus, today I decree my deliverance by fire by force in the name of Jesus. By the power of your word today, I violently decree my deliverance from negative dreams and nightmares in the name of Jesus. From today and forevermore, no force of darkness, entities, witchcraft power, voodoo, or any form of power of darkness will have any access to my dreams in the name of Jesus. Your word says that the kingdom of God suffers violence and it is only the violent that takes it by force. Today Lord, I take my deliverance by fire and by force from negative dreams and nightmares in the name of Jesus. Amen.

Negative Dreams and Nightmares

Dear Lord, I lose every band of captivity that has held me bound in my dreams in the name of Jesus. I, therefore, decree that I am set free from every power of darkness by force today in the name of Jesus. No power of hell or principalities of darkness will ever torment me or afflict me in my dreams in the name of Jesus, Amen.

Father today I make demands for my deliverance by force in the name of Jesus. You have stated in your word that on that day shall the burden of negative dreams and nightmares be lifted off my shoulders because the yoke of negative dreams and nightmares shall be destroyed because of the anointing. Lord, by the reason of the anointing today all forms of negative dreams and nightmares, every form of marine influence in my dreams, every sort of demonic oppression in the night, and everything that is contrary to the word of the Lord, today I decree that they are destroyed by the reason of the anointing in the name of Jesus. Therefore, the yoke of negative dreams and nightmares are broken forever by the power of the anointing in the name of Jesus. Amen.

Father your word says a time is coming that I will gain the dominion and because of the dominion that I will gain, I will be able to break the yoke of negative dreams and nightmares off my neck. Father today I have gained that dominion by the word of the Lord and have decreed and declared that I am free from every form of oppression in the night in the name of Jesus. No longer will the devil have access to my dreams again in the name of Jesus.

John 8:36

> ***If the Son therefore shall make you free, ye shall be free indeed.***

Negative Dreams and Nightmares

Holy Father, I come to you today by the power of your word. Your word says, whosoever that the son of man shall make free, that person is free indeed not with any form of conditionality attached to it. Lord Jesus because you have made me free from bad dreams and nightmares, today, I decree my liberty in the name of Jesus and I am free indeed.

Enforcing peaceful night Rest

Psalms 127:2

> *It is vain for you to rise up early, to sit up late, to eat the bread of sorrows: <u>for so he giveth his beloved sleep.</u>*

Psalms 4:8

Pius Joseph

I will both lay me down in peace, and sleep: for thou, Lord, only makest me dwell in safety.

Father in the mighty name of Jesus, I approach the throne of grace boldly to enforce your word that says you are the one that gives onto your children peaceful sleep. Satan does not give sleep and he can never give me sleep. If he does not have the power to give sleep, then he does not have the power to interrupt with that which you have given unto me. I, therefore, stand by the power of your word, and I decree that my sleep from henceforth shall be peaceful in the name of Jesus. I, therefore, pray that I will sleep like a baby and wake up like a baby without any form of terrifying dreams or nightmares.

Negative Dreams and Nightmares

Father in the mighty name of Jesus, I make demands for the enforcement of safety in my dreams in the name of Jesus. I lay down to sleep because it is only you that can make me dwell safely in my sleep in the name of Jesus. I ask that may I dwell safely in my sleep in the mighty name of Jesus, thank you mighty father. In the name of Jesus, Amen.

Father in the name of Jesus, I make demands for sound sleep on the authority of the Scriptures under reference in the name of Jesus. It is your will that my sleep is devoid of every form of harassment and intimidation from the kingdom of darkness, marine influences, witchcraft operations, occult powers, by the authority in the mighty name of Jesus, Amen.

Binding the Spirit of Fear and Disfavour

Lord Jesus, today I bind every spirit of fear that the enemy must have put into my heart because of the nightmares and dreams I have been having in the name of Jesus. Your word says that he that fears is not perfected in love. I stand by the authority of the word of God because you have not given me the spirit of fear or bondage but of love, power, and self-discipline. Therefore, I curse every spirit of fear that the enemy has placed into my life in the name of Jesus. I command him to depart out of my life in the name of Jesus, amen.

Father in the name of Jesus, anything that the enemy might have used my dream to cause disfavour in my life in the physical, I stand today by the authority of your word and I decree it is canceled and annulled in the name of Jesus. As I go out today to do activities that I am supposed to do, I will walk in your favour in the mighty name of Jesus.

Father in the name of Jesus, I make demands today for the cancellation of the works of darkness in my life in the name of Jesus.

Negative Dreams and Nightmares

Every spirit of rejection which the enemy has used bad dreams and nightmares to place into my life, I decree and declared that the spirit of rejection is removed out of my life in the name of Jesus. Your word has said, that everything that you have not planted, it shall be removed from its roots in the name of Jesus. Therefore, I stand by the authority of your word and I declare the removal of everything that the enemy has used my dreams to plant into my life in the name of Jesus.

Matthew 13:25

> *But while men slept, his enemy came and sowed tares among the wheat, and went his way.*

Lord, by the power and the authority of your word, everything that the enemy might have used the dream of the night in order to sowed tares into my life, I make demands today for the removal of those tares in the name of Jesus. I thank you because I know it is done, in the name of Jesus. Amen.

Father in the mighty name of Jesus, every form of sex that I have had in the dreams that have caused the exchange of my life and destiny, today I decree the cancellation of that in the name of Jesus. You have said in your word that you will restore unto us all the years that the caterpillar, the Palmer worm, and cankerworm have eaten you will restore it. I, therefore, make demands for the restoration of the dreams and plans you have for my life in the name of Jesus.

Father in the mighty name of Jesus, if by the reason of any sexual interaction in my dreams, the enemy has used that opportunity to steal anything in my life, I command the restoration of it in the mighty name of Jesus. I stand by the authority of

Negative Dreams and Nightmares

your word that says whenever a thief is caught, he shall restore sevenfold. Therefore, everything that belongs to me is restored back in the name of Jesus.

Lord, everything I have eating in my dream that has cost me to lose financial favour or caused general disfavour in my life, today I nullify the power of that food that I have eaten in my dream in the name of Jesus, Amen.

Heavenly Father, I know that I ought not to be ignorant of the devices of the enemy. Sometimes the enemy can use my own dreams in other to give me food to eat so that I can be sick. Therefore anything that I have eaten in the dreams that have the capacity to cause anything to me, today I nullify it and convert it to become nutritious to my body in the name of Jesus.

Pius Joseph

Prayer of appreciation

1 John 5:14-15

> *And this is the confidence that we have in him, that, if we ask any thing according to his will, he heareth us:*
>
> *15 And if we know that he hear us, whatsoever we ask, we know that we have the petitions that we desired of him.*

Psalms 103:1-2

> *Bless the Lord, O my soul: and all that is within me, bless his holy name.*

Negative Dreams and Nightmares

2 Bless the Lord, O my soul, and forget not all his benefits:

3 Who forgiveth all thine iniquities; who healeth all thy diseases;

4 Who redeemeth thy life from destruction; who crowneth thee with lovingkindness and tender mercies;

5 Who satisfieth thy mouth with good things; so that thy youth is renewed like the eagle's.

Dear Lord, I come here to thank you for the answers to all of my prayers above. This is the greatest confidence I have in you that whenever I come before you with my prayer request, you always listen to me. Your ears are constantly open to the cry of the righteous. Thank you, father, because you have heard me and answered my petitions, in the name of Jesus, Amen.

Father, I want to thank you for the blood of your son which is now standing as the solid defence in my dream, barring the devil from having access to me when I sleep in the name of Jesus. Thank you, dear Lord, for this wonderful thing that you have done, in Jesus name, Amen.

Heavenly Father, I want to appreciate you for rebuilding my hedge and creating a wall of fire around my sleep. I know Lord by the reason of what you have done, I will no longer have negative dreams or nightmares. The devil ceases to have any form of access to defile me while I sleep through sex, marine influences, eating in the dream of the night,

Negative Dreams and Nightmares

or having to see strange animals chasing me in my dream. To you be all the glory, and honour in the mighty name of Jesus.

Finally, Lord, I want to thank you for activating these scriptural truths in my life that you give unto your children peaceful sleep and that you make all of your children to dwell safely in the night. Daddy, I am aware that from tonight, my sleep will be without any form of tormenting dreams or nightmares in the mighty name of Jesus. Thank you mighty father for the fulfillment of the Scriptures in my life. I glorify your name, in the name of Jesus

If you are reading this book and you are not saved, pray this prayer after me:

Lord Jesus, I come before you today. I give you my heart. I give you my all. Come into my life. Become my Lord and saviour. Deliver me from the power of sin. Help me to live for you forever, in Jesus name.

Prayer

Let us know about your prayer needs as our team add you to our prayer list and intercede fervently on your behalf.

Also, check our blog for Holy Ghost inspired contents.

www.thetentofglory.com

Negative Dreams and Nightmares

I would love to hear from you how our ministry and our books have blessed you. Write to us at

pius@thetentofglory.com

Our Books

1.   Interpretation of Tongues: Be Filled with the Spirit, Unlock Speaking in Tongues & Know What You Are Praying

2.   The Keys to Fervent Prayer: The Prayer Warrior Guide to Praying Always

3.   How to make the Holy Ghost Your Closest Friend (Book 2)

4.   The Holy Spirit Friendship Manual: How to make the Holy Ghost Your Close Friend (Book 1) (Free-EBook)

5. Walking in the Path of Divine Direction Always

6. The Expediency of Tongues:

7. Breaking Soul Ties the Simple Way: How to Break Soul Ties and Receive Freedom

8. How to Read the Bible And Understand It

9. BAPTISM OF THE HOLY SPIRIT: Easy Steps to be Filled With the Holy Spirit And Obtain the Gifts of the Holy Spirit

10. Prayer That Never Fails

11. Vision from The Heavenly

12. Baptism of the Holy Ghost Prayer Book: How to Minister the Baptism of the Holy Ghost to yourself and others.

13. How to Hear God's Voice: A Believer's Manual For Talking with God

Negative Dreams and Nightmares

14. Guide to Effective Fasting and Praying: A Way of Fasting And Prayers That Guarantee Results

Printed in Great Britain
by Amazon